Klick! 5

Englisch

Erarbeitet von
Nicola Göbels,
Berit Rudolph

Cornelsen

Klick! Englisch 5

Erarbeitet von
Nicola Göbels, Köln; Berit Rudolph, Lüneburg

Beratende Mitwirkung
Volker Blechschmidt, Völklingen; Gundula Brüning, Dortmund; Renate Fölster-Kretschmann, Freudenstadt; Ilka Kirchhoff, Hagen am Teutoburger Wald; Anna Meißner, Darmstadt; Jens Otte, Berlin; Melitta Sahak, Paderborn; Amke Wolbert, Ladenburg

Verlagsredaktion
Marie Keenoy, Susanne Döpper (Projektleitung); Caroline Huy, Michaela Schmidt, Silja Wollburg

Illustration
Carlos Borrell, Berlin (S. 4, 5 Landkarte); Kate Davies, Wiltshire, England (S. 42, 43 Cartoon); Stephen Elford, East Sussex, England; Heidi Kull, Zeichnerei Kull, Berlin; Simon Rumble, Beehive Illustration, Cirencester, England

Gesamtgestaltung
Klein & Halm Grafikdesign, Berlin

Bildquellen
Alamy, Abingdon (S. 18 u. m.: All Canada Photos; S. 24 u. l.: Megapress; S. 26 o. r.: Alan Howden - Australia Stock Photography; S. 32 o. l.: Wildlight Photo Agency; S. 32 o. r.: Bill Bachman; S. 32 u. l.: Tibor Bognar; S. 34 o. l.: Friedrich Stark; S. 34 o. r.: Image Source; S. 34 u. l.: Associated Sports Photography; S. 38 o.: StockImages); Jan Bornebusch, Berlin (S. 13 u.); Cinetext, Frankfurt a. M. (S. 44 o. r., u. l.: Sony Pictures Ent./Cinetext; S. 44 u. r.: Sony Pictures/Cinetext); Cornelsen Archiv, Berlin (S. 45 Szene: Corel Library); Getty Images, München (S. 10 o. l.: DreamPictures; S. 11 date: Dimitri Vervitsiotis); iStockphoto, Calgary (S. 7 Zugspitze: Photo75; S. 11 party: james steidl; S. 12 u. l.: Colleen Butler; S. 12 u. r.: Kevin Russ; S. 18 o. l.: Steve Froebe; S. 18 u. r.: Lauri Patterson; S. 19 hospital: Jesper Elgaard; S. 19 flower shop: Joe Potato Photo; S. 19 florist: Edyta Pawlowska; S. 19 care assistant: Dean Mitchell; S. 21 u.: Ron Brancato; S. 24 o. l.: Adam Booth; S. 24 o. r.: Jerry Moorman; S. 27 save: redmal; S. 27 eat well: Olga Lyubkina; S. 27 babysit: Alex Gumerov; S. 29 u.: Chris Schmidt; S. 35 get married: Skip ODonnell; S. 38 u. r.: Steven Miric; S. 40 o. l.: uros ravbar; S. 40 o. r. elephant: Johan Swanepoel; S. 40 o. r. rhino: Eric Isselée; S. 40 o. r. buffalo: Jonathan Heger; S. 46 Junge links: Edyta Pawlowska; S. 46 BLT: Kelly Cline; S. 49 Junge: Juanmonino); Picture-Alliance, Frankfurt a. M. (S. 16 u. l.: Akg-images; S. 40 u. l.: Graeme Williams; S. 45 Figuren: Picture Press/Wartenberg, Frank P.); Shutterstock, New York (S. 3, 5, 7, 9 Globus: Alex Staroseltsev; S. 3, 11, 13, 15, 17 Flagge: Arteki; S. 3, 19, 21, 23, 25 Flagge: Fotogroove; S. 3, 27, 29, 31, 33 Flagge: sjgh; S. 3, 35, 37, 39, 40, 41 Flagge: Andrew Chin; S. 3, 43, 45 Buch: Pshenichka; S. 3, 47, 49 Würfel: Gjermund Alsos; S. 7 Brandenburger Tor: Tobias Machhaus; S. 7 Rhein: ultimathule; S. 10 u. l.: Chris Hellyar; S. 10 u. r.: Paul Prescott; S. 11 best friends: michaeljung; S. 11 boy/girlfriend: hartphotography; S. 11 u., S. 14: holbox; S. 15 cricket: Kenneth William Caleno; S. 16 o. l.: Rafal Cichawa; S. 16 o. r.: De Visu; S. 18 o. r.: Paul McKinnon; S. 18 u. l.: fstockfoto; S. 19 on time: Villiers Steyn; S. 19, 48 polite: James Peragine; S. 19 dressed properly: Elnur; S. 19, 48 hard-working: Maksymilian Skolik; S. 26 o. l.: Brooke Whatnall; S. 26 u. l., u. r.: Debra James; S. 27 spend: Diego Cervo; S. 27 don't smoke: Yobidada; S. 27 do sport: Kitch Bain; S. 27 don't drink: Tatiana Popova; S. 27 do the washing: Dusan Zidar; S. 27 u.: Ian Scott; S. 34 u. r.: Only Fabrizio, Reproduction authorised by the South African Reserve Bank; S. 35 bathroom: JirkaBursik; S. 35 living room: Phase4Photography; S. 35 kitchen: Henrik Winther Andersen; S. 35 clothes: Grin Maria; S. 35 stay single: Yuri Arcurs; S. 35 have children: Supri Suharjoto; S. 37 boy: Andrejs Pidjass; S. 38 u. l.: Poznyakov; S. 40 o. r. leopard: Magdalena Bujak; S. 40 o. r. lion: geraldb; S. 46 Junge rechts: Suzanne Tucker; S. 46 u. r.: Edyta Pawlowska; S. 47 u.: Ronen; S. 48 Sheila: Catalin Petolea; Silja Wollburg, Berlin (S. 10 o. r.); worldofstock.com (S. 26 o. m.: Dennis MacDonald)

Lied- und Textquellen
S. 16: Zitat von Mahatma Gandhi mit freundlicher Genehmigung von GandhiServe - www.gandhiserve.org; S. 24: Rap: Canada; S. 32: Rap: Australia; S. 40: Poem: Nelson Mandela: lyrics by Michael Vaughan-Rees; S. 45 adaptiert von Jennifer Seidl. A New Life Down Under. Cornelsen English Library - Fiction. Berlin: Cornelsen, 2007.

www.cornelsen.de

1. Auflage, 1. Druck 2011

Alle Drucke dieser Auflage sind inhaltlich unverändert und können im Unterricht nebeneinander verwendet werden.

Druck: CS-Druck CornelsenStürtz, Berlin

ISBN 978-3-06-031937-4

Inhalt gedruckt auf säurefreiem Papier aus nachhaltiger Forstwirtschaft.

Inhaltsverzeichnis

English around the world

People speak English in these countries.

1 Listen and repeat. Find the places on the map.

1.2

→ AH S. 3

2 a) Look and listen.

1.3

Samir Liam Olivia Megan

b) Listen again and take notes. Tell a partner about the teenagers.

1.3

name: Samir
country: India
age: 16
hobbies: basketball

Samir is from India.
He's 16.
He likes basketball.

c) Tell a partner about yourself.

→ AH S. 4

3 a) Find the USA and Great Britain on the map.

b) Read and say. What's American? What's British?

school uniforms	baseball	pounds	Queen Elizabeth
dollars	Barack Obama	Red Nose Day	Thanksgiving

- Thanksgiving **is** American.
- Pounds **are** British.

→ AH S.5

4 Ask and answer in your class.

– What languages do you speak?
– Where do people speak the languages?

Tipp:
Schlage die Namen der Sprachen und Länder im Wörterbuch oder im Internet nach.

English around the world

1 a) Listen and read.

1.4

Big C's Fan Club

calendar | photos | fan chat

Liam4Ca Sunday, August 7th, 10:57	I just bought Big C's new CD. The song "You're the one" is so cool! Do you think any songs are better?
Oly5Australia Sunday, August 7th, 10:59	Yes, I think the song "K1" is cooler than "You're the one". It's the coolest song on the CD.
Samir6India Sunday, August 7th, 11:05	I agree, Oly5Australia. "You're the one" is good, but "K1" is better. I think "Waking up" is the best song on the CD.
Meg9SAfrica Sunday, August 7th, 11:09	Big C's next concert is in Cape Town and I'll be there! I think "You're the one" is Big C's best song. I love it!

b) Complete the sentences.

- Liam thinks the song "K1" is … than "You're the one".
- Samir thinks "You're the one" is …, but "K1" is …
- Samir thinks "Waking up" is … song on the CD.

Tip:
good → better → the best

→ AH S. 6

2 English in Germany: Work with a partner.

a) Jens doesn't understand everything. Help him in German.
b) Think of more places where you see or hear English in Germany.

→ AH S. 7

Learning English

Gruppenarbeiten mit neuen Medien präsentieren

1. Vorbereitung:
   - Bildet Dreiergruppen.
   - Sucht im Internet die folgenden Informationen zu einem Land eurer Wahl: die Sprache, die Hauptstadt, einen Berg, einen Fluss, eine Sehenswürdigkeit.
   - Gestaltet dazu eine Bildseite mit dem PC.
   - Schreibt einen Text mit dem PC.
   - Teilt den Text so auf, dass jeder aus der Gruppe etwas sagt.

language: German
capital: Berlin
mountain: Zugspitze
river: Rhein
sight: Brandenburger Tor

GERMANY

Brandenburger Tor in Berlin

Zugspitze

Rhein

We want to tell you about Germany.
In Germany people speak German.
The capital of Germany is Berlin.
The Zugspitze is a big mountain. A long river is the Rhein.
We think tourists should see the Brandenburger Tor in Berlin.

2. Vortrag:
   - Schlagt das Arbeitsheft auf Seite 9 auf.
   - Projiziert die Bilder mit einem Beamer an die Wand.
   - Sprecht den Text laut und deutlich. Seht dabei eure Zuhörer an.

Tipp:
Ihr könnt die Bildseite auch auf Folie ausdrucken und an die Wand projizieren.

→ AH S. 9

English around the world

1 Cartoon: Read and act it out.

1.5

2 What's a good title for the cartoon?

- Holidays in Germany
- Camping in Cornwall
- A trip to South Wales

3 Read and answer.

a) Where is Cornwall?
b) Why are Kevin and Jenny in Cornwall?
c) Why do they speak English first?

→ AH S. 8

4 Talk about English in your class.

When do you need English?

- I need English …

→ on holidays • for surfing the Internet • for listening to music • for flirting • for my dream job • at the airport • ?

New words

any	irgendwelche
Australia	Australien
Canada	Kanada
country	Land; (ländliche) Gegend
do the dishes	Geschirr spülen
Great Britain	Großbritannien
holiday	Ferien; Urlaub
India	Indien
Ireland	Irland
just	gerade (eben)
language	Sprache
love	Liebe; lieben
not	nicht
same	gleich
school trip	Klassenfahrt
South Africa	Südafrika
speak	sprechen
United States of America (USA)	Vereinigte Staaten von Amerika
who	wer

Speaking English

So steigerst du kurze Adjektive:

- cool – cool**er** – the cool**est**
- **good** – **better** – the **best**

So kannst du mit kurzen Adjektiven Dinge miteinander vergleichen:

- The song "You're the one" is **cool**, but "K1" is **cooler**.
- "Waking up" is **the coolest** song.
- "K1" is **cooler** than "You're the one".

→ Die Steigerungsformen aller Adjektive in diesem Buch findest du in der Wörterliste auf S. 51–56.

Unit 1
Love & friendship

1 **a) Look at the pictures about love and friendship in India.**

b) Find India on the map on pages 4 and 5.

a

Bollywood film

b

Indian wedding

c

cricket

d

eating chicken curry

2 **Look, listen and answer.**

1.6

- Put the pictures in the right order.
- Name three activities that Samir likes doing.
- What do you find out about Bollywood?
- What colour are wedding dresses in India?

3 **Ask and answer with a partner.**

What's your favourite film?

My favourite film is …

→ sport • food • song

4 **a) Listen and repeat.**

1.7

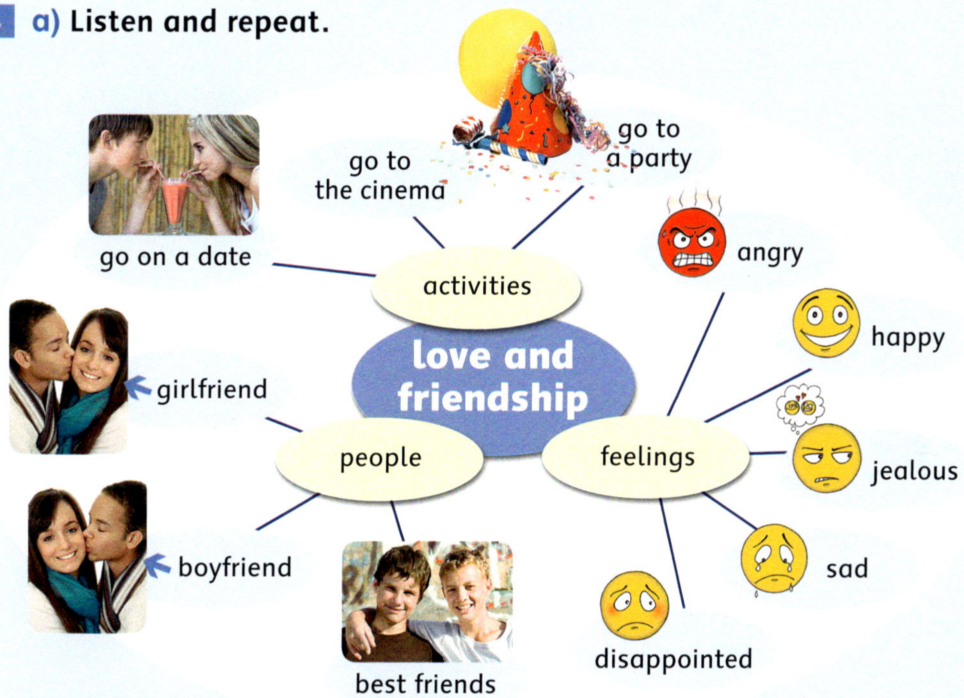

→ AH S. 11

b) Think of more activities. Write in your exercise book.

5 **a) Listen and read.**

1.8

Tip:
him = ihn
her = sie

Rania: I'm so angry.
Lisa: Why?
Rania: Yesterday I wanted to go to the cinema with Ralph. But he wasn't there.
Lisa: Why not? What did he say?
Rania: He said: "I can't go, my head hurts." Then I saw him in town with Sarah.
Lisa: That's bad. He isn't a good boyfriend. You should talk to him about it.
Rania: You're right.

→ AH S. 12

b) Act it out with a partner. Use your dialogue card.

→ AH DK 1

Love & friendship

1 **a) Listen to Rupesh and Dave.**

1.9

b) Tell a partner about your dream girlfriend, boyfriend or best friend.

– He/She ... → listens to me • is often happy • is never angry • makes me laugh • likes going to parties • ?

– He/She has ... → brown hair • blue eyes • short hair • ?

– He's/She's ... than me. → older • taller • shorter • ?

→ AH S. 13

2 **Listen and act it out with a partner.**

1.10

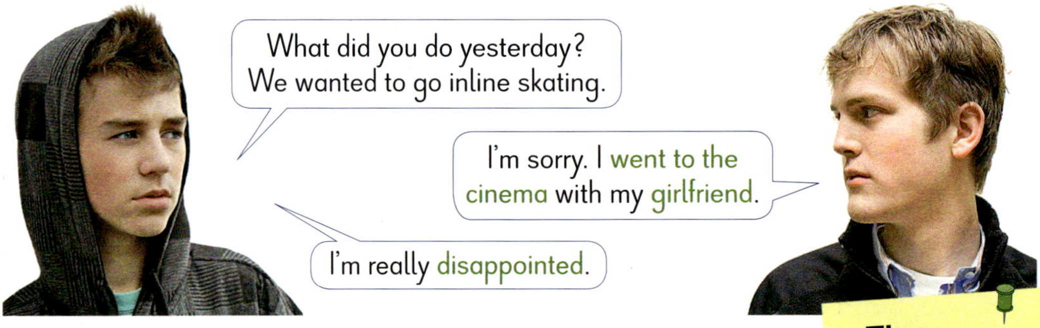

→ jealous • angry • sad

→ go shopping • watch TV • go to a party • play computer games

→ boyfriend • best friend

Tipp:
In diesem Band musst du die richtige Form der Verben bilden, bevor du sie einsetzt. Hier z. B.:
go → went
watch → watched

→ AH S. 14

3 a) **Listen and read.**

1.11

Dear Anita,

We met at sports day last week. We talked about school and films. We found out that we like the same films. Horror films are so cool! Do you know who I am? I'm the boy with the short brown hair and the green eyes. I wore blue shorts and a red T-shirt. I really liked talking to you. Would you like to go to the cinema with me next Friday? Call me at 0112468. Hope to talk to you before Friday.

Love, Rupesh

Tip:
meet → met
find → found
wear → wore

b) **Write a letter in your exercise book.**

Learning English

Wörter mit Karteikarten üben

1. Schreibe das deutsche Wort auf die Vorderseite einer Karteikarte und die englische Übersetzung auf die Rückseite.
2. Sieh dir das deutsche Wort auf der ersten Karte an.
3. Wenn du die englische Übersetzung weißt, lege die Karte auf einen Stapel. Weißt du sie nicht, lege die Karte auf einen zweiten Stapel.
4. Nimm den zweiten Stapel und übe die Wörter, bis du alle kannst.
5. Übe alle Wörter regelmäßig, täglich 5 bis 10 Minuten. Du kannst auch mit einem Partner lernen. Fragt euch gegenseitig ab.

→ AH S. 17

Love & friendship

1 Listen and read.

1.12

Have a problem? Ask Miranda!

Dear Miranda,

I'm so angry at my friend Lisa. She wrote bad things about me on our online social network. She wrote: "Anita is so crazy. She's the craziest girl at school." Everybody can read it! I think Lisa is jealous because she likes my boyfriend. What should I do?

Anita, 16

Dear Anita,

First you should block Lisa on your online social network. Send an e-mail to the network and say what she wrote. Then tell your mother, your father or a teacher. They'll help you.

Yours, Miranda

2 Read and answer.

a) What's Anita's problem?
b) Why is Lisa jealous?
c) What should Anita do?

Tip:
crazy → crazier → the craziest

3 Talk to a partner.

– A German friend has the same problem as Anita. What does Miranda say? Tell your friend in German.

→ AH S. 15

4 Ask and answer in groups: How often do you chat online?

1. Copy the chart. Ask and tick.
   - I never chat online.
   - I chat online once a week.
2. Present the answers to the class:
   - Tom never chats online.
   - Betty and Mike chat online once a week.

	never	once a week	twice a week	three times a week
Tom	✓			
Betty		✓		
Mike		✓		
...				

1 Cartoon: Read and act it out.

1.13

→ AH DK 2

2 Find a title for the cartoon. You can use a dictionary.

3 Complete the sentences.

a) Samir is happy to be alone because …
b) Samir thinks girls are … because they only talk about …
c) Tyler lives in … Samir lives in …
d) Tyler wants to … Samir in the …

→ AH S. 16

India

1 **Read and answer.**

1.14

True friendship comes when silence between two people is comfortable.

Mahatma Gandhi

Tip:
Go to www.cornelsen.de.
Type in the webcode:
KLEN319374-16.

- What does this mean in German? Use a dictionary for help.
- Do you know this feeling? Do you think this is true friendship?

2 **Look and listen.**

1.15

Many tourists go to India to see the famous Taj Mahal. Some people think it's a palace, but it isn't. It's a grave. A very rich man built it for the woman he loved. The Taj Mahal is now over three hundred years old.

a) What's the Taj Mahal?
b) Who built the Taj Mahal?
c) How old is the Taj Mahal?

→ AH S. 16

Im Vergleich zu anderen Ländern ist Indien sehr dicht bevölkert. Heute leben etwa eine Milliarde Menschen dort. Bis 1947 stand Indien unter britischer Herrschaft. Deshalb spricht man dort heute noch Englisch. Mahatma Gandhi setzte sich für die Unabhängigkeit Indiens ein und wurde zu einem großen Vorbild für sein Volk. Er war gegen jede Form von Gewalt. Im Jahr 1948 wurde Gandhi erschossen. Seine Lehre der Gewaltlosigkeit wird weiterhin von vielen Menschen verehrt.

New words

alone	allein
always	immer
angry	wütend
bad	schlecht
block	blockieren, sperren
boyfriend	fester Freund
crazy	verrückt
disappointed	enttäuscht
everybody	alle; jeder
feeling	Gefühl
friendship	Freundschaft
girlfriend	feste Freundin
go on a date	ein Date haben
happy	glücklich
jealous	eifersüchtig
look at	ansehen
online social network	soziales Netzwerk im Internet
our	unser, unsere
sad	traurig
say	sagen
town	Kleinstadt; Stadt
young	jung

Speaking English

Jemanden beschreiben:

- He has black hair and brown eyes. He's taller than me.
- He's never jealous.

Fragen und sagen, was man gemacht hat:

- What **did** you do yesterday?
  – I **went** inline skating with my girlfriend.

→ More Reading S. 42–43 • Extra Practice S. 47

Unit 2
Work

1 **a) Look at the pictures about work in Canada.**

b) Find Canada on the map on pages 4 and 5.

a

fishermen

b

police officers in Canada (Mounties)

c

professional ice hockey player

d

maple syrup farm

e

pancakes with maple syrup

2 **Look, listen and answer.**

1.16

- What jobs do a lot of people do in Canada?
- What does Liam want to be?
- What's a Mountie?

3 **Project: Make and present a poster about jobs in your town.**

- This is a poster about jobs in Wolfsburg.
- There are a lot of car mechanics in Wolfsburg. There are …

4 a) Listen and repeat.

1.17

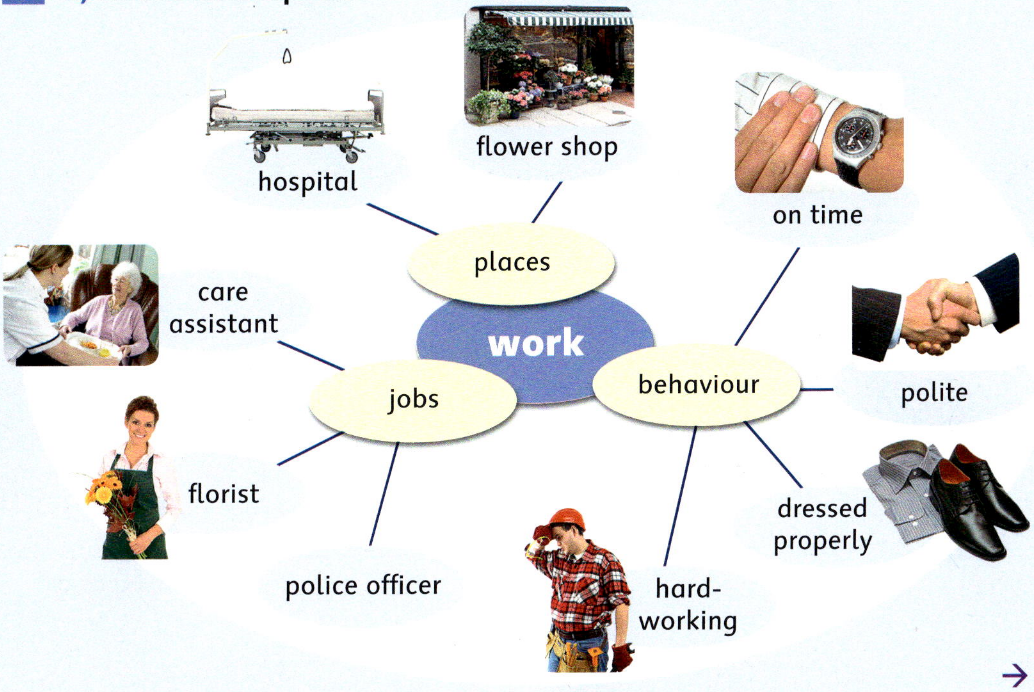

→ AH S. 19

b) Think of more places. Write in your exercise book.

5 a) Listen and read.

1.18

Sue: Why aren't you at the hospital?

Jake: I can't do the last week of my work experience. My boss sent me home.

Sue: Why? What did you do?

Jake: I wasn't on time on Monday and Tuesday.

Sue: Oh, Jake, you should always be on time at your work experience.

Jake: I know. I really want to be a care assistant.

Sue: You should talk to our teacher.

→ AH S. 20

b) Act it out with a partner. Use your dialogue card.

→ AH DK 3

Work

1 **a) Listen to Mr Jones and Calvin.**

1.19

b) Ask and answer with a partner.

– Where do you want to work?

→ hospital • zoo • ?

→ zoo keeper • care assistant • ?

– Why should you get the job?

→ working with tools • working in a team • writing • talking to people • ?

→ always on time • always dressed properly • hard-working • ?

→ AH S. 21

2 **a) Listen and say it with a partner.**

1.20

b) Tell a partner about Bill's day.

Bill is a … He gets up at …

→ AH S. 22

Tipp:
In englischsprachigen Ländern wie Kanada fügt man dem Lebenslauf kein Foto bei.

3 a) Listen and read.

1.21

Name:	Amy Baker
Address:	67 Spring Street, Ottawa, ON, K1N 6N5, Canada
E-mail:	amy@ca
Phone number:	(613) 379-468
School:	York Street High School, class 9a
Job experience:	work experience at a baker's shop for 3 weeks; part-time job at Hip Shop
Languages:	English, French
Hobbies:	swimming, fashion

b) Write this text about yourself. You should use a computer.

Learning English

Einem Sachtext genaue Informationen entnehmen

1. Welche Art von Text hast du vor dir?
   (z. B. Bericht, Stellenanzeige, Werbung, Zeitungsartikel)
2. Lies den Text einmal ganz durch.
3. Überlege, was du wissen möchtest. Fragen helfen dir:
   What? Where? When? Who? Why?
4. Lies den Text noch einmal. Suche nach Antworten und notiere sie.
5. Wenn du ein Wort nicht verstehst, schlage es im Wörterbuch nach.
6. Lies den folgenden Text und wende die Schritte 1.–5. an.

Jay's Carpentry
We have a position available for work experience as a carpenter.
Your working hours will be from eight o'clock to four o'clock.
You can start on November 15th.
Please contact us at JsShop@ca.

→ AH S. 25

Work

1 Listen and read.

1.22

Amy Baker
67 Spring Street
Ottawa, ON, K1N 6N5
E-mail: amy@ca
Tel: (613) 379-468

Cool Fashion
Linda Brown
137 East Street
Ottawa, ON, K1N 6N5

August 18th, 2012

Dear Mrs Brown,

I am writing about your job advert for a shop assistant. I did my work experience at a baker's shop. Last summer I had a part-time job at Hip Shop.

I am good at talking to people and I like fashion. I am very polite, always on time and hard-working. I am good at working in a team and I would like to be on your team. I can start on October 1st.

Yours sincerely,

Amy Baker

2 Read and answer.

a) Who is looking for a new shop assistant?
b) Where does Amy want to work?
c) What part-time job did Amy have last summer?
d) Why should Amy get the job?
e) When can Amy start the job?

→ AH S. 23

3 Ask and answer in your class.

a) Would you like to work in a shop? Why? Why not?
b) Did you do work experience? Where?
c) What are you good at?

4 Look at exercise 1 and write a letter in your exercise book.

1 Cartoon: Read and act it out.

1.23

→ AH DK 4

2 Find a title for the cartoon. You can use a dictionary.

3 Talk about the cartoon in your class.

- What did Liam do right?
- What should you check before a job interview?
- What would you wear for a job interview?
- What wouldn't you wear for a job interview?

→ AH S. 24

Canada

1 Rap: Canada

1.24

From Québec in the East
To Vancouver in the West,
Every Canadian thinks
Their city is the best.

You can see bears and fish
In the forests and the lakes,
Or eat pancakes with syrup
And really awesome steaks.

2 Look and listen.

1.25

Tip:
Go to www.cornelsen.de.
Type in the webcode:
KLEN319374-24.

There are beautiful landscapes in Canada. The Niagara Falls are big waterfalls between Canada and the USA. You can take a tour on a boat to see them. Logging is a big industry in Canada because there are a lot of forests there.

a) Where are the Niagara Falls?
b) What can you do at the Niagara Falls?
c) What's a big industry in Canada?

→ AH S. 24

Kanada ist ein Einwanderungsland. Aus vielen Ländern kommen Menschen nach Kanada, um dort zu leben und zu arbeiten. Daher werden in Kanada viele Sprachen gesprochen. Es gibt sogar zwei offizielle Landessprachen: Englisch und Französisch. Ungefähr ein Viertel der Kanadier spricht Französisch als Muttersprache. Québec ist ein Gebiet im Osten Kanadas. Hier spricht die Mehrheit der Menschen Französisch und alle Verkehrsschilder sind auf Französisch. Was bedeutet „arrêt" wohl auf Deutsch?

New words

advert	Anzeige
behaviour	Benehmen
care assistant	Pfleger/in
carpenter	Schreiner/in
dressed properly	angemessen gekleidet
early	früh
florist	Florist/in
flower shop	Blumenladen
French	Französisch
hard-working	fleißig
hospital	Krankenhaus
job experience	Berufserfahrung
job interview	Bewerbungsgespräch
look	aussehen
on time	pünktlich
other	andere, anderer, anderes
police officer	Polizist/in
polite	höflich
start	anfangen
Yours sincerely	Mit freundlichen Grüßen

Speaking English

Fragen und sagen, warum etwas passieren sollte:

- **Why** should you get the job?
  – **Because** I'm good at talking to people.

Fragen und sagen, was man regelmäßig macht:

- What do you do every day?
  – I have a shower at six o'clock.

Sagen, was jemand anderes regelmäßig macht:

- Bill goe**s** to school at 7.30.

→ More Reading S. 44 • Extra Practice S. 48

Unit 3
Teen life

1 **a) Look at the pictures about teen life in Australia.**
b) Find Australia on the map on pages 4 and 5.

a

voluntary work with koalas

b

Don't drink at the beach.

c

surfers at the beach

d

Great Barrier Reef

e

Sydney on the east coast

2 **Look, listen and answer.**

2.1

- Put the pictures in the right order.
- What can you do in your free time in Australia?
- What shouldn't you do at the beach in Australia?

3 **Ask and answer in groups. Use a dictionary.**

- What voluntary work can you do in your town?
- What voluntary work would you like to do? Why?

4 a) Listen and repeat.

2.2

→ AH S. 27

b) Think of more jobs you do at home. Write in your exercise book.

5 a) Listen and read.

2.3

Tim: Hi, May. How are you?
May: I'm so angry.
Tim: Why?
May: My mum always says: Don't smoke, eat well! Do this, do that … blah, blah, blah.
Tim: My mum is the same. What do you have to do today?
May: I have to do the washing.
Tim: OK, I'll help you. Let's go to the cinema after that … or eat some healthy fruit?
May: Ha! Ha! But thank you, Tim.

→ AH S. 28

b) Act it out with a partner. Use your dialogue card.

→ AH DK 5

Teen life

1 a) Listen to Peter and Olivia.

2.4

b) Ask and answer with a partner.

– You look great today, … How do you do it?

– I … → eat fruit and vegetables every day • drink enough water • do sport three times a week • don't smoke • go outdoors every day • ?

– I really have to … → eat more fruit and vegetables • drink more water • do more sport • stop smoking • go outdoors more • ?

→ AH S. 29

2 Listen and say it with a partner.

2.5

→ go to the park • go to the cinema • go to a party • play basketball • go to a rugby match • go shopping • ?

→ do my homework • clean the kitchen • help our grandmother • do the washing • cook dinner • ?

→ AH S. 30

3 a) Listen and read.

2.6

Oly5Australia	I went to the Great Barrier Reef last weekend. It was a great trip. You should really go and see it.
Sid9	Hi, that's great! In my next holidays I want to go to the Great Barrier Reef too. What should I take with me?
Oly5Australia	You should take suncream because most days you'll be outdoors. It can be very hot. Take flip-flops for sunny days. You should take a sweatshirt too. It can be cold when it's rainy. Take a book for rainy days, and a jacket. Oh, and you should take a cap for sunny days.
Sid9	Thanks for helping me!

b) What should Sid9 take? Make a list in your exercise book.

→ AH DK 6

sunny days	rainy days
suncream	book
...	...

Learning English

Nachfragen bei Verständnisproblemen

1. Wenn du in einem Gespräch etwas nicht verstehst, solltest du gezielt nachfragen.
2. Folgende Sätze können dir in so einer Situation helfen:
   Can you say that again, please?
   Can you speak slowly, please?
   What does ... mean?

3. Wenn du nachgefragt hast, ist es wichtig, deiner Gesprächspartnerin gut zuzuhören und selbst deutlich zu sprechen.

→ AH S. 33

Teen life

1 Look and listen.

2.7

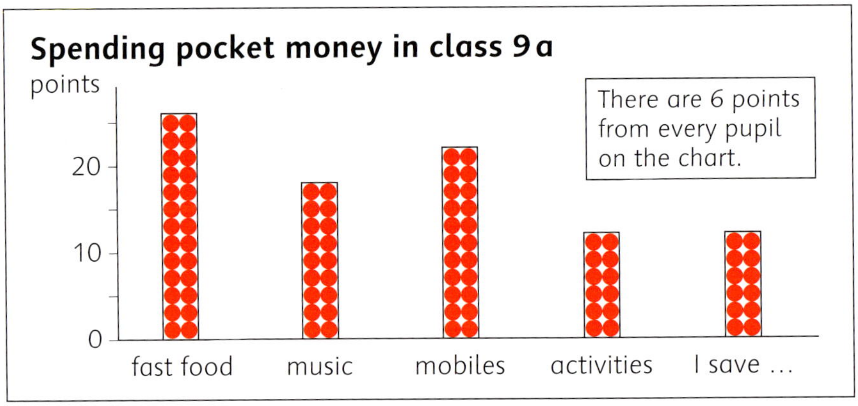

2 Read and answer.

a) What's the chart about?
b) How many pupils are there in class 9 a?
c) What do the pupils spend their pocket money on?
  – The pupils spend a lot of their pocket money on …
  – The pupils save … of their pocket money.

→ some • most

3 Talk about the chart in groups.

I think the pupils shouldn't spend so much of their pocket money on …

I agree.

I don't agree.

→ AH S. 31

4 Project: How do you spend your pocket money?

1. Write down three things from the chart.
   Draw your points next to them.

   ● 1 point for spending some of your pocket money
   ●● 2 points for spending a lot of your pocket money
   ●●● 3 points for spending most of your pocket money

2. Make a chart with every pupil's points and talk about it.

We save some of our pocket money.
We spend a lot of our pocket money on …

1 Cartoon: Read and act it out.

2.8

Tipp:
Christmas = Weihnachten
In Australien ist in der Weihnachtszeit Sommer.

2 Find a title for the cartoon. You can use a dictionary.

3 Look at the cartoon and make a list in your exercise book.

healthy	not healthy
eat well	...
...	...

→ AH S. 32

4 Find the song "Rudolph, the Red-Nosed Reindeer"on the Internet.

Australia

1 Rap: Australia

2.9

A barbecue's a barbie,
'Good morning' is 'g'day',
My friends are my cobbers,
And footy's what we play.
Here in Australia
We like to drink and eat,
Outdoors with my cobbers
We have barbies for the meat.

2 Look and listen.

2.10

Tip:
Go to www.cornelsen.de.
Type in the webcode:
KLEN319374-32.

The outback is a dry, hot landscape in the middle of Australia. Many people in the outback live on farms far from cities, schools and hospitals. Most pupils in the outback learn at home. Their teachers give lessons online.

a) What's the outback?
b) What's special about school in the outback?
c) How do the pupils in the outback get lessons?

→ AH S. 32

Die Ureinwohner Australiens werden Aborigines genannt. Traditionell leben sie in Einklang mit der Natur. Der Ayers Rock ist für die Aborigines ein heiliger Ort. Sie nennen ihn Uluru. Über der Erdoberfläche ist er 348 m hoch, unter der Erde 6000 m tief. Der Fels ist von vielen Höhlen durchzogen. Weil es auf seiner Oberfläche viele Wasserlöcher gibt, umgibt Uluru fruchtbares Land in der sonst trockenen Landschaft.

New words

after that	danach
alcohol	Alkohol
babysit	babysitten
do the washing	Wäsche waschen
eat well	gesund essen
for	für
health	Gesundheit
healthy	gesund
ice cream	(Speise-)Eis
later	später
life	Leben
more	mehr
most	meiste, meisten
nose	Nase
pocket money	Taschengeld
point	Punkt
smoke	rauchen
spend	ausgeben
suncream	Sonnenschutzcreme
that	das
their	ihr, ihre
this	diese, dieser, dieses

Speaking English

Sagen, was man machen muss:

- I **have to** drink more water.

Sagen, was man gerade macht:

- I'm help**ing** my mum.

Sagen, was jemand anderes gerade macht:

- She's help**ing** her mum.

→ More Reading S. 45 • Extra Practice S. 49

Unit 4
Future plans

1 a) Look at the pictures about Megan's future plans in South Africa.

b) Find South Africa on the map on pages 4 and 5.

a

township in Cape Town

b

Kruger National Park

c

rugby

d

South African money (Rand)

2 Look, listen and answer.

2.11

- Where does Megan want to do voluntary work?
- What's her dream job?
- What does Megan want to do with her pocket money?

3 Talk to a partner. Think of two questions you want to ask Megan.

- Is there basketball in South Africa?
- Are there mountains in South Africa?

4 a) Listen and repeat.

2.12

→ AH S. 35

b) Think of more things you'll need money for. Write in your exercise book.

5 a) Listen and read.

2.13

Megan at age 26:

Megan: Oh Jim, look at this cool mobile.
Jim: It's really cool, but we can't buy it. We have to save money for our new kitchen.

Megan: Yes, I know.
Jim: Come on, let's look for a fridge.

Megan: We need a washing machine too.
Jim: Yes, and the baby needs a warm jacket.

Megan: Bye bye, cool mobile.

→ AH S. 36

b) Act it out with a partner. Use your dialogue card.

→ AH DK 7

Future plans

2.14 **1 a) Listen to Megan and Jim.**

Tip:
I'd = I would

b) Ask and answer with a partner.

– What kind of flat would you like?

→ with a very big living room • with big windows • with a lot of light • with a dishwasher • with a new kitchen • not far from the train station • ?

→ AH S. 37

2.15 **2 a) Listen and match the text on the CD to the pictures.**

b) Ask and answer with a partner.

– What are your future plans, …?
– I think I'll …
I don't think I'll …
I hope I'll …
What about you?

→ live in a small town. • have a car. • work as a … • have children. • live in a big city. • live in a house. • get a good job. • have a flat. • get married. • stay single. • ?

→ AH S. 38

3 a) Listen and read.

2.16

I'm looking for a nice flat:

Nice flat in Cape Town, not far from a train station and a supermarket • big living room with big windows and a lot of light • two bedrooms • kitchen with washing machine and dishwasher • modern bathroom with shower • no more than 600 Rand a week (with water and electricity).

Please call me: 021352468

b) Write an advert for your dream flat in your exercise book.

c) Draw and label your dream flat. Present it to the class.

My dream flat has a big kitchen with modern technology. It has …

→ AH DK 8

Learning English

2.17

Einem Hörtext wichtige Informationen entnehmen

1. Überlege zuerst, welche Art von Text du hörst. Ist es z. B. eine Durchsage am Bahnhof, eine Mailbox-Nachricht oder ein Radiospot?
2. Du musst nicht jedes Wort verstehen. Achte auf Wörter, die du kennst.
3. Achte auf wichtige Informationen, z. B. Nummern, Daten, Uhrzeiten und Namen.
4. Notiere die wichtigen Informationen auf einem Notizblock.
5. Hör dir nun den Track 2.17 auf der CD an und wende die Schritte 1.–4. an.

(1)
Flight: …
Gate: …

→ AH S. 41

Future plans

1 Listen and read.

2.18

My hopes and worries for the future

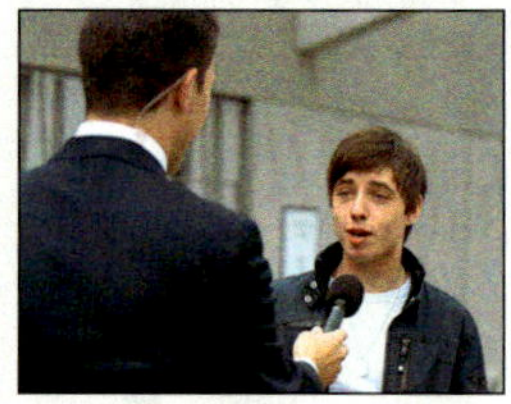

Ben is in his last year at Mandela School. A reporter from "Teenage Life" talked with him about his hopes and worries for the future.

Reporter: *Ben, what will you miss after school?*
Ben: I'll miss my friends and one or two of my teachers.
Reporter: *What are your worries for the future?*
Ben: I'm worried I won't get my dream job. I want to be a carpenter.
Reporter: *What are your biggest hopes for the future?*
Ben: I hope I'll visit Kruger National Park and see the animals there. I also hope I'll earn enough money because I want to have a family with children and live in a nice flat.
Reporter: *Thank you for the interview, Ben. Good luck for the future!*

2 Read and answer.

a) What will Ben miss after school?
b) What are his worries for the future?
c) What does Ben want to do in the future?
d) Does he want to stay single?

→ AH S. 39

3 Project: Make a poster and present it.

- What will you miss after school?
- What are your biggest hopes for the future?

Tipp:
Du kannst Bilder aus Zeitschriften und Katalogen benutzen.

My future

I'll miss my school friends.

I hope I'll live in a nice flat.

1 Cartoon: Read and act it out.

2.19

2 Work with a partner. Find a title for the cartoon.

3 Match the sentences and write them in your exercise book.

1 First …	a … Jim talks about his future as a big boss.
2 Then …	b … Megan laughs at Jim because he's late.
3 After that …	c … Jim and Megan look at great houses.

4 Talk about the cartoon in your class.

I think Jim will be very rich.

I agree.

I don't agree.

→ AH S. 40

South Africa

1 Poem: Nelson Mandela

2.20

Mandela helped black South Africans who wanted to be free.
He fought so blacks and whites could live together happily.
For this he went to prison in 1964.
He stayed in prison for 20 years and more.
They made him president of South Africa in 1994.
People round the world will love him now and forever more.

2 Look and listen.

2.21

Tip:
Go to www.cornelsen.de.
Type in the webcode:
KLEN319374-40.

The landscape in South Africa is beautiful. Many tourists visit the country to go on a safari. Park rangers show tourists the wild animals in the national parks. Leopards, elephants, lions, rhinos and buffalos are very famous. People call them the 'Big Five'.

a) What do many tourists do in South Africa?
b) What are the 'Big Five'?
c) Where do they live?

→ AH S. 40

In Südafrika herrschte sehr lange Rassentrennung (Apartheid) zwischen schwarzen und weißen Einwohnern. Viele Menschen kämpften dagegen. Besonders berühmt wurde Nelson Mandela. 1964 wurde er wegen seines Kampfes gegen die Apartheid verurteilt und musste bis 1990 im Gefängnis bleiben. Für seinen Einsatz für Gleichberechtigung bekam Mandela 1993 den Friedensnobelpreis. Er wurde 1994 der erste schwarze Präsident Südafrikas.

New words

bathroom	Badezimmer
children	Kinder
clothes	Kleidung
company	Firma
flat	Wohnung
future (plans)	Zukunft(spläne)
get married	heiraten
Good luck!	Viel Glück!
hope	Hoffnung; hoffen
house	Haus
late	verspätet
learn	lernen
living room	Wohnzimmer
maybe	vielleicht
miss	vermissen; verpassen
of	von
rich	reich
stay single	ledig bleiben
worry	Sorge; sich Sorgen machen

Speaking English

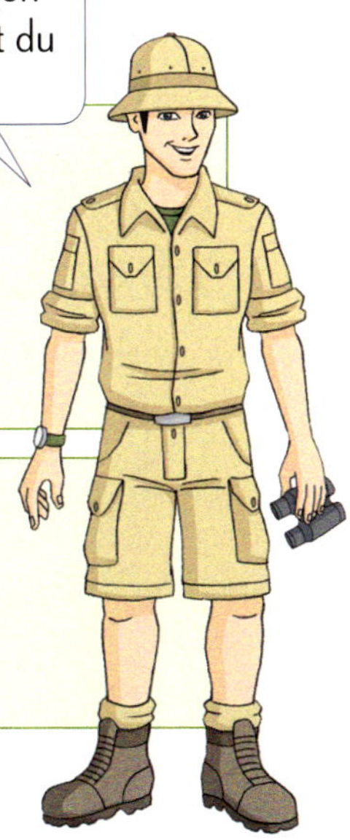

Fragen und sagen, welche Art von Wohnung man gerne hätte:

- What kind of flat would you like?
  – I'd like a flat with a living room and a modern bathroom.

Fragen und sagen, wie man sich die Zukunft vorstellt:

- What are your future plans?
  – I think **I'll** get married. I hope **I'll** have a nice flat.

→ More Reading S. 46 • Extra Practice S. 50

More Reading: Unit 1

1 **Read and act it out.**

2.22

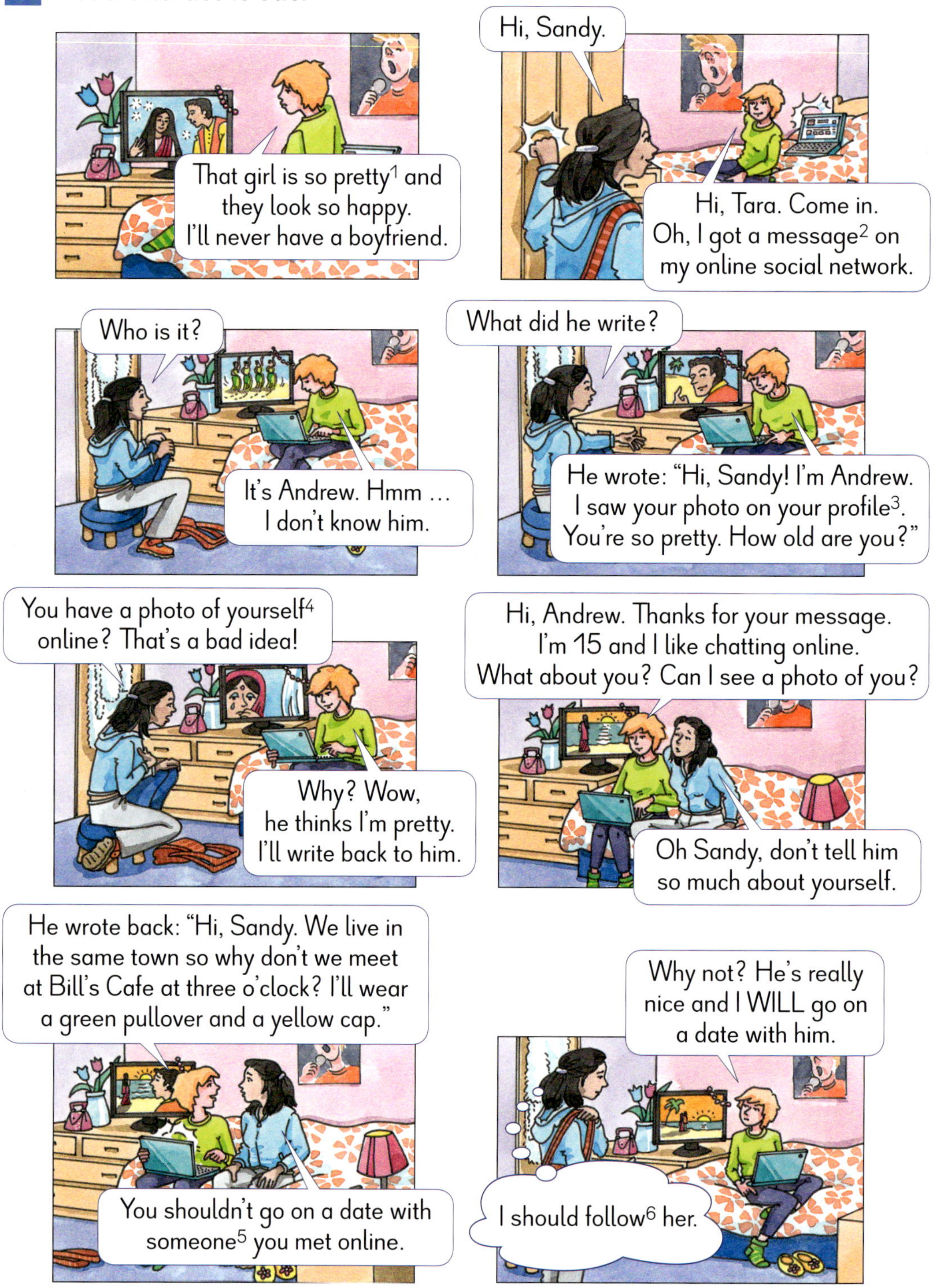

[1]hübsch [2]Nachricht [3]Profil [4]dir [5]jemandem [6]folgen [7]Polizei

2 **a) Write down the words you don't understand in your exercise book.**
b) Work with a partner. Write the words in German. You can use the word list or a dictionary.

3 **Match and write the sentences in your exercise book.**

1. First Sandy was sad because …
2. Then she was happy because …
3. Tara was worried because …
4. Sandy was happy because …

→ Sandy wanted to go on a date with Andrew. • she didn't have a boyfriend. • Tara was at the cafe too. • Andrew sent her a message.

4 **What do you think about Sandy and Tara? Talk with a partner.**

I think Sandy …

I think Tara …

→ had too much on her profile. • was right. • was clever. • is a good friend. • had a good idea. • ?

→ AH S. 43–44

More Reading: Unit 2

1 Listen and read.

2.23

The film "The Pursuit of Happyness" is a true story about the salesman[1] Chris Gardner. In 1981 he lives in San Francisco with his wife[2], Linda and his son[3], Christopher. When he loses[4] a lot of money and his job, his wife leaves him and their son.

Chris wants to find a new job. He does work experience in a big bank, but he doesn't earn money for six months[5]. He hopes he'll get a job in the bank after that, but he doesn't know. Chris and his son lose their flat because Chris can't pay[6] for it.

But Chris never gives up[7]. He wants to be a good father. At work he's always friendly and dressed properly. He's very good at talking to people and he's hard-working.

After the hardest[8] six months of his life, Chris gets the job. He's very happy. Years later Chris Gardner is the boss of a company and is very rich.

[1] Vertreter [2] Ehefrau [3] Sohn [4] verliert [5] Monate [6] bezahlen [7] gibt nie auf [8] härtesten

2 What would they say? Look at the pictures and act it out with a partner.

3 Work in groups. Talk about the film.

1. Write questions about the film on cards. The words "When? What? Where? Who? Why?" can help you.
2. Then ask and answer the questions in your class.

Where do the Gardners live?

→ AH S. 45–46

More Reading: Unit 3

1 **a) Look at the cover and guess. What's the book about?**
b) Listen and read.

2.24

Alice looked at her room. All her books, photos and posters were no longer there. The house looked cold and empty[1]. She was sad. She didn't want to leave England, her home and her friends. Her dad had a new job in Sydney, Australia, so the family had to go there too. But why so far away?

On the flight, Alice took out her blue notebook[2]. Telephone numbers, e-mail addresses and photos of all her friends were in there. She was homesick[3], but her family was happy about the new experience[4].

"I'll tell you about Sydney," her younger brother Jeff said and opened a book. "'Sydney is the capital of New South Wales. It's one of the most beautiful[5] cities in the world[6] with its harbour[7].' That sounds[8] great!" Jeff looked at Alice and asked, "Alice, are you listening?" Alice said, "I hope ..."

[1] leer [2] Notizbuch [3] hatte Heimweh [4] Erfahrung [5] schönsten [6] Welt [7] Hafen [8] Das klingt ...

2 **Match the sentences.**

1 She's homesick.
2 It's a beautiful city.
3 Sydney is a new experience for Jeff.

a It's a nice city.
b It's his first time in Sydney.
c She wants to be at home.

3 **Read and write in your exercise book. Who is who?**

a) He gets a new job in Sydney. – It's ...
b) He thinks Sydney is great. – It's ...
c) She doesn't want to leave England. – It's ...

4 **Write an ending in your exercise book. Act it out with a partner.**

– Alice: I hope ...
– Jeff: Don't worry, Alice. ...

→ I'll like the new school. • my friends from home will write soon. • ?

→ You'll find friends soon. • Everything will be fine. • It'll be great. • ?

→ AH S. 47–48

More Reading: Unit 4

1 a) Listen and read.

b) Match the pictures to the text.

2.25

1. Cook two slices of bacon in a pan.
2. Cut up some lettuce and one tomato.
3. Toast two slices of bread.
4. Put two tablespoons of mayonnaise on the slices of toast.
5. Put the lettuce, tomato and bacon on one slice of toast.
6. Put the other slice of toast on top. Now you have a BLT.

c) Work with a partner.

a) Write the text in German in your exercise book.
   You can use a dictionary.

b) Why is the sandwich called a BLT?

2 a) Talk about your favourite sandwiches in a group.

→ chicken • sausage • tomato • banana • honey • ?

b) Write a shopping list for your group's favourite sandwich. → AH S. 49

Extra Practice: Unit 1

1 John only speaks English. Tim only speaks German. Act it out in groups.

John: Let's watch a film with, oh, I don't know his name! He has short blond hair and blue eyes. He's from the USA. He's often in action films.

Lucy: Hmm. Tim, wir wissen nicht, wie dieser Schauspieler heißt. Er hat …

Tim: Ich glaube, er meint …

→ AH S. 50, Nr. 1

2 a) Think of a star you like. Write six things in the mind map in your exercise book. You can use a dictionary.

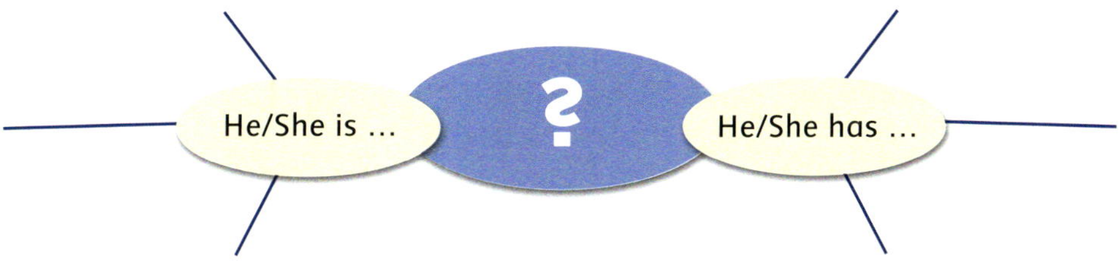

b) Tell a partner about your star. Listen to your partner and guess.

3 What does Shin say? Write in your exercise book.

Yesterday after school, I had lunch and I … my homework. Then I … TV. But it … boring. So I … my friend Mike on his mobile. Mike … at our school and he … to play basketball with Joel, Tina and Mary. But they weren't there! So I … my basketball and … to school. We … basketball for an hour. Then we … in the park. We … about school and sports.

→ be (2x) • call • chill out • do • go • play • take • talk • want • watch

→ AH S. 50, Nr. 2

Extra Practice: Unit 2

1 Describe a typical day at your work experience.

1. Find words for your text. Listen to the words in an online dictionary and repeat them.
2. Make a list in your exercise book.

Job: cook	
What do you do?	What do you need?
• cook • clean • …	• food • dishwasher • …

3. Write five sentences in your exercise book about a typical day at your work experience. Read them to a partner.

   – I get up at … o'clock. Then I go to …

Tip:
Look at page 20 for help.

→ AH S. 51, Nr.

2 a) Look at the pictures and write in your exercise book.

Dan says: "Every year on my mum's birthday we/she …"

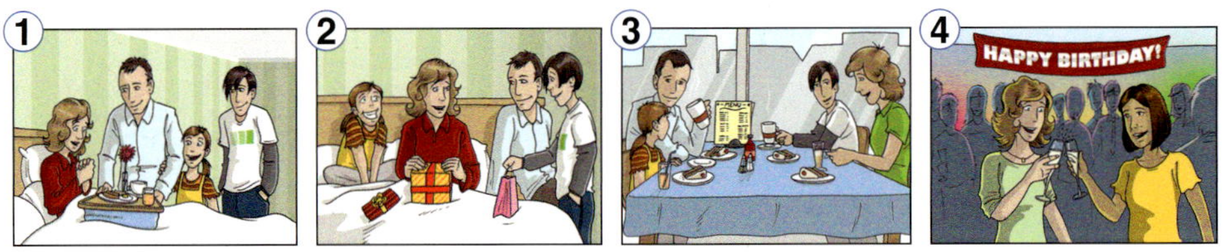

we … she … we … she …

→ get presents • watch TV • make breakfast for her • have a party • go to a cafe

b) Write about your birthday in your exercise book.

→ AH S. 51, Nr.

3 Look and write in your exercise book.

Sheila wants to be a florist. Why should she get the job?
– Because …

→ AH S. 51, Nr.

Extra Practice: Unit 3

1 a) Read about Ben's Sundays.

I really don't like Sundays! I have too much to do. My mum and my dad always need my help at home. Every Sunday, I have to walk the dog. I have to do the washing too. I babysit my brother and we visit my grandmother. I'm happy when it's Monday.

b) Write about Ben's Sundays in your exercise book.

– Ben really doesn't like Sundays. He …

→ AH S. 52, Nr. 1

2 a) Look and write in your exercise book. Use the "-ing" form.

a) Two boys are playing basketball.

b) A boy …
c) A teacher …
d) A girl …
e) A girl and a boy …
f) Two painters …

→ paint a house • do their homework • listen to music • read a book • babysit his sister • watch the basketball game • ?

b) Look again and write three more sentences in your exercise book.

→ AH S. 52, Nr. 2

3 a) Write three sentences about a picture in Unit 3 in your exercise book. You can use a dictionary.

b) Tell a partner. Listen and guess.

A girl is sitting in a classroom.

Is it on page 27?

Extra Practice: Unit 4

1 a) Write in your exercise book.

– What kind of films do you like?
– I like action films.

b) Now ask and answer with a partner.

2 a) Maria doesn't speak German. Lisa doesn't speak English. Act it out in groups.

Maria: Hi, Ben. Hi, Lisa. What would you like to do today?
Ben: Maria möchte wissen …
Lisa: Ich würde gerne zum Strand gehen und windsurfen. Was möchte Maria denn gerne machen?
Ben: Lisa would …
Maria: I'd like to relax on the beach and have an ice cream.
Ben: Maria würde gerne …

→ AH S.53, Nr.

b) Write three sentences in your exercise book about your dream holidays.

– I'd like to snowboard in the mountains.

→ relax • meet • go • visit • have • stay • surf • camp • ?

→ nice people • at/to the beach • parties • in a hotel • in a city • ?

3 a) What does Bob say? Look and write in your exercise book.

b) Write about Bob's future in your exercise book.

– Bob thinks he'll … – Bob thinks he won't …

→ AH S.53, Nr

Wörterliste

Wörter, die mit einem kleinen Kringel (°) markiert sind, gehören nicht zum Lernwortschatz.
In der Wörterliste sind alle Verben in Klammern auch in der Vergangenheit angegeben.
Bei allen Adjektiven sind in Klammern die Steigerungsformen angegeben.

A

a, an ein, eine
about über
accent Akzent
activity Aktivität
address Adresse
advert Anzeige
after nach
after that danach
against gegen
age Alter
agree (agreed) zustimmen
airport Flughafen
alcohol Alkohol
alone allein
always immer
and und
angry (→ angrier → angriest) wütend
animal Tier
any irgendwelche
apple Apfel
April April
arm Arm
arrive (arrived) ankommen
Art Kunst
at an; bei; um
August August
aunt Tante
Australia Australien
awards show Preisverleihung

B

babysit (babysat) babysitten
back Rücken; zurück
bad (→ worse → worst) schlecht
bag Tasche
baker Bäcker/in
banana Banane
barbecue Grillparty
basketball Basketball
bathroom Badezimmer
be (was, were) sein
beach Strand
bear Bär
°**beautiful (→ more beautiful → most beautiful)** schön
because weil
bed Bett
bedroom Schlafzimmer
before vor
behaviour Benehmen
best beste, besten
better besser
°**between** zwischen
big (→ bigger → biggest) groß
big wheel Riesenrad
bike Fahrrad
birthday Geburtstag
black schwarz
block (blocked) blockieren, sperren
blond blond
blue blau
°**boat** Boot
body Körper
book Buch
boring (→ more boring → most boring) langweilig
boy Junge
boyfriend fester Freund
bread Brot
breakfast Frühstück
brother Bruder
brown braun
budgie Wellensittich
°**buffalo** Büffel
°**build (built)** bauen
bus Bus
bus station Busbahnhof
bus stop Bushaltestelle
but aber
butter Butter
buy (bought) kaufen
Bye. Tschüss!

C

cafeteria Kantine
call (called) anrufen; nennen
camp (camped) zelten
can (could) können; dürfen
Canada Kanada
cap Kappe
capital Hauptstadt
car Auto
car mechanic Automechaniker/in
care assistant Pfleger/in
carpenter Schreiner/in
carry (carried) befördern; tragen
castle Burg; Schloss
cat Katze
cereal Frühstücksflocken
chair Stuhl
chart Diagramm
chat online (chatted online) im Internet chatten
check in/out (checked in/out) ein-/auschecken
cheese Käse
children Kinder
chill out (chilled out) sich ausruhen; entspannen
chips Pommes frites
cinema Kino
class Klasse
classroom Klassenzimmer
clean (cleaned) aufräumen; putzen
clothes Kleidung
club Arbeitsgemeinschaft
cold (→ colder → coldest) kalt
colour Farbe
come (came) kommen
company Firma
concert Konzert
construction worker Bauarbeiter/in

controller Eingabegerät für Computerspiele
cook (cooked) Koch/Köchin; kochen
country Land; (ländliche) Gegend
cousin Cousin/e
crazy (→ crazier → craziest) verrückt
cupboard Schrank

D

dance (danced) tanzen
day Tag
December Dezember
digital camera Digitalkamera
dinner Abendessen
disappointed (→ more disappointed → most disappointed) enttäuscht
dishwasher Geschirrspüler
do (did) machen, tun
do the dishes (did the dishes) Geschirr spülen
do the washing (did the washing) Wäsche waschen
dog Hund
door Tür
double room Doppelzimmer
download (downloaded) herunterladen
drama club Theater AG
dream Traum
dressed properly angemessen gekleidet
drink (drank) trinken
°**dry (→ drier → driest)** trocken
DVD-player DVD-Spieler

E

eagle Adler
early (→ earlier → earliest) früh
earn (earned) verdienen
east Osten
eat (ate) essen
eat well (ate well) gesund essen
egg Ei
electricity Elektrizität
°**elephant** Elefant
England England
enough genug
every jede, jeder, jedes
everybody alle; jeder
Excuse me. Entschuldigung.
eye Auge

F

family Familie
famous (→ more famous → most famous) berühmt
far (→ farther → farthest) weit weg
°**farm** Farm
farm worker Gehilfe/in in der Landwirtschaft
father Vater
favourite Lieblings-
February Februar
feeling Gefühl
felt tip Filzstift
find (out) (found (out)) (heraus)finden
fine in Ordnung
finger Finger
first erst; zunächst
fish Fisch; angeln
flat Wohnung
flat screen TV Flachbildfernseher
flight Flug
florist Florist/in
flower shop Blumenladen
folder Mappe
food Essen
foot Fuß
football Fußball; American Football
for für
forest Wald
French Französisch
Friday Freitag
fridge Kühlschrank
friend Freund/in
friendship Freundschaft
from aus; von
fruit Obst
funny (→ funnier → funniest) lustig
future (plans) Zukunft(spläne)

G

game Spiel
garden Garten
gardener Gärtner/in
Germany Deutschland
get (got) bekommen; kommen
get married (got married) heiraten
get up (got up) aufstehen
ghost Geist
girl Mädchen
girlfriend feste Freundin
give (gave) geben
glue Kleber
go (went) gehen
go on a date (went on a date) ein Date haben
golden aus Gold; golden
good (→ better → best) gut
Good luck! Viel Glück!
Good morning. Guten Morgen.
Goodbye. Auf Wiedersehen.
grandfather Großvater
grandmother Großmutter
°**grave** Grab
great (→ greater → greatest) toll
Great Britain Großbritannien
green grün
guinea pig Meerschweinchen
guitar Gitarre
gym Sporthalle

H

hair Haare
hairdresser Friseur/in
ham Schinken
hamster Hamster
hand Hand
handbag Handtasche
happy (→ happier → happiest) glücklich
hard-working (→ more hard-working → most hard-working) fleißig
have (had) haben
have to (had to) müssen
he er
head Kopf
health Gesundheit
healthy (→ healthier → healthiest) gesund
help (helped) helfen
her ihr, ihre
here hier
Here you are. Hier bitte.
his sein, seine
History Geschichte
holiday Ferien; Urlaub
home Zuhause
homework Hausaufgaben
honey Honig; Liebling
hope (hoped) Hoffnung; hoffen
hospital Krankenhaus
hot (→ hotter → hottest) heiß
house Haus
how wie
hungry (→ hungrier → hungriest) hungrig
hurry (hurried) sich beeilen
hurt (hurt) wehtun

I

I ich
ice cream (Speise-)Eis
idea Idee
in in
India Indien
indoors drinnen
°**industry** Industrie
inline skate (inline skated) inlineskaten
into in
invent (invented) erfinden
Ireland Irland
it es
IT PC-Unterricht

J

jacket Jacke
January Januar
jealous (→ more jealous → most jealous) eifersüchtig
job experience Berufserfahrung
job fair Jobmesse
job interview Bewerbungsgespräch
juice Saft
July Juli
June Juni
just gerade (eben)

K

keep (kept) behalten
key Schlüssel
kick (kicked) treten
kind Art; Sorte
kitchen Küche
knee Knie
know (knew) kennen; wissen

L

lake See
landscape Landschaft
language Sprache
last letzte, letzter, letztes
late (→ later → latest) spät; verspätet
laugh (laughed) lachen
lead Leine
learn (learned) lernen
leave (left) etwas zurücklassen
left links
leg Bein
lend (lent) leihen
°**leopard** Leopard
°**lesson** Unterrichtsstunde
Let's ... Lass uns ...
life Leben
lifeguard Rettungsschwimmer/in
light Licht
like (liked) mögen; wie
°**lion** Löwe
listen (listened) hören; zuhören
live (lived) leben
living room Wohnzimmer
°**logging** Holzfällen
long (→ longer → longest) lang
look (looked) aussehen
look at (looked at) ansehen
look for (looked for) suchen
lorry driver LKW-Fahrer/in
lot: a lot (of), lots (of) eine Menge, viele
love (loved) Liebe; lieben
lunch Mittagessen

M

magazine Zeitschrift
make (made) machen
°**man** Mann
many viele
map Karte
March März
marmalade Orangenmarmelade
Maths Mathematik
May Mai
maybe vielleicht
me mich; mir
meet (met) (sich) treffen
memory stick USB-Stick
microwave Mikrowelle
°**middle** Mitte
milk Milch
minute Minute

miss (missed) vermissen; verpassen
mobile Handy
Monday Montag
money Geld
more mehr
most meiste, meisten
mother Mutter
mountain Berg
mountain bike Mountainbike
mouse Maus
much viel
music Musik
my mein, meine

N

name (named) Name; nennen
°**national park** Nationalpark
need (needed) brauchen
never nie
new (→ newer → newest) neu
newspaper Zeitung
next nächste, nächster, nächstes
nice (→ nicer → nicest) nett
no nein
north Norden
nose Nase
not nicht
November November
now jetzt
number Zahl

O

October Oktober
of von
often oft
old (→ older → oldest) alt
on auf; an
on time pünktlich
once einmal
onion Zwiebel
online social network soziales Netzwerk im Internet
only nur
or oder
orange Orange; orange
other andere, anderer, anderes
our unser, unsere
°**outback** Outback
outdoors draußen
oven Ofen
°**over** über

P

painter Maler/in
°**palace** Palast
park ranger Parkaufseher/in
parking space Parkplatz
part-time job Teilzeitjob
path Pfad
pen Füller
pencil Bleistift
pencil case Federmäppchen
people Menschen
perfect perfekt
pet Haustier
photo Foto
photocopier Kopierer
pick up (picked up) aufheben
picture Bild; Foto
pink pink; rosa
place Ort
plant Pflanze
play (played) spielen
please bitte
pocket money Taschengeld
point Punkt
police officer Polizist/in
polite (→ more polite → most polite) höflich
postcard Postkarte
pound (£) Pfund
present Geschenk
presentation Präsentation
problem Problem
projector Beamer
pub Kneipe, Lokal
pupil Schüler/in

Q

quick (→ quicker → quickest) schnell

R

rabbit Kaninchen
radio Radio
rainy (→ rainier → rainiest) regnerisch
rat Ratte
read (read) lesen
real echt
really wirklich
red rot
relax (relaxed) sich entspannen
°**rhino(ceros)** Nashorn
rich (→ richer → richest) reich
right rechts; richtig
ringtone Klingelton
river Fluss
robot Roboter
roll Brötchen
room Raum
rubber Radiergummi
rubbish Müll
rule Regel
ruler Lineal

S

sad (→ sadder → saddest) traurig
°**safari** Safari
same gleich
sandy (→ sandier → sandiest) sandig
Saturday Samstag
sausage Würstchen
save (saved) sparen; speichern
say (said) sagen
school Schule

school trip Klassenfahrt
Science Naturwissenschaften
score Ergebnis
secret Geheimnis
security guard Sicherheitsbedienstete/r
see (saw) sehen
See you (later). Bis später. / Tschüs.
send (sent) schicken
September September
she sie
shelf Regal
shoe Schuh
shop (shopped) Geschäft; einkaufen
shop assistant Verkäufer/in
short (→ shorter → shortest) kurz
should sollen
shoulder Schulter
°**show (showed)** zeigen
shower Dusche
sing (sang) singen
single room Einzelzimmer
sister Schwester
ski (skied) Ski; Ski fahren
skirt Rock
sleep (slept) schlafen
small (→ smaller → smallest) klein
smoke (smoked) rauchen
snake Schlange
snowboard (snowboarded) Snowboard; snowboarden
sock Socke
some (→ more → most) einige; etwas
sometimes manchmal
song Lied
Sorry. Tut mir leid.
south Süden
South Africa Südafrika
speak (spoke) sprechen
spend (spent) ausgeben
Sport Sport
start (started) anfangen
state Staat
stay (stayed) bleiben
stay single (stayed single) ledig bleiben
stomach Bauch; Magen
straight along geradeaus
street Straße
subject Unterrichtsfach
summer Sommer
suncream Sonnenschutzcreme
Sunday Sonntag
sunny (→ sunnier → sunniest) sonnig
supermarket Supermarkt
surf (surfed) wellenreiten
swim (swam) schwimmen
swimming pool Schwimmbad

T

table Tisch
table tennis Tischtennis
tackle (tackled) angreifen
take (took) andauern; machen; nehmen
talk (talked) sprechen
tall (→ taller → tallest) groß
tea Tee
teacher Lehrer/in
technology Technologie
tell (told) erzählen
text (texted) Text; eine SMS schicken
than als
Thank you. / Thanks. Danke.
that das
the der, die, das
their ihr, ihre
°**them** sie
then dann
there dort
there is/are … es gibt …
they sie
thing Ding
think (thought) denken; meinen
this diese, dieser, dieses
three times dreimal
throw (threw) werfen
Thursday Donnerstag
time Uhrzeit; Zeit
tired (→ more tired → most tired) müde
to nach; zu
today heute
tomato Tomate
tomorrow morgen
too auch; zu
tool Werkzeug
touch screen Berührungsbildschirm
tour Reise; Tour
tourism Tourismus
°**tourist** Tourist/in
town Kleinstadt; Stadt
traffic (jam) Verkehr(sstau)
train Zug
train station Bahnhof
trip Fahrt
trousers Hose
Tuesday Dienstag
turn (turned) abbiegen
turn on (turned on) anmachen
turtle Schildkröte
TV Fernseher
twice zweimal

U

uncle Onkel
under unter
United States of America (USA) Vereinigte Staaten von Amerika
use (used) benutzen

V

vegetable Gemüse
very sehr
visit (visited) besuchen

W

wait (waited) warten
wake up (woke up) aufwachen
walk (walked) laufen
want (wanted) wollen
wash (washed) waschen
washing machine Waschmaschine
watch (watched) sich anschauen
water Wasser
°**waterfall** Wasserfall
way Weg
we wir
wear (wore) anhaben, tragen
webcam Webcam
website Website
Wednesday Mittwoch
week Woche
weekend Wochenende
welcome willkommen
west Westen
what was
when wann
where wo
white weiß
who wer
why warum
°**wild (→ wilder → wildest)** wild
will werden
window Fenster
windsurf (windsurfed) windsurfen
with mit
°**woman** Frau
work (worked) Arbeit; arbeiten
work experience Betriebspraktikum
worry (worried) Sorge; sich Sorgen machen
would würden
write (wrote) schreiben

Y

°**year** Jahr
yellow gelb
yes ja
yesterday gestern
you du; Sie
young (→ younger → youngest) jung
your dein, deine
Yours sincerely Mit freundlichen Grüßen

Z

zoo keeper Tierpfleger/in